Follow The
FOOD
CHAIN

Who Ate the Snake?

A DESERT FOOD CHAIN

Sarah Ridley
Crabtree Publishing Company
www.crabtreebooks.com

CRABTREE
PUBLISHING COMPANY
WWW.CRABTREEBOOKS.COM

Author: Sarah Ridley

Editorial director: Kathy Middleton

Editors: Nicola Edwards, Ellen Rodger

Proofreader: Crystal Sikkens

Designer: Lisa Peacock

Prepress technician: Samara Parent

Print coordinator: Katherine Berti

Photo credits:

iStock: BLFink 17c; CochiseVista 16c, 17bcr, 19br, 21cr; Frank Fitchmüller front cover br, 15c, 15bc, 17bc, 19bc, 21b; Mary F Wilber 19.
Nature PL: John Cancalosi 8c, 13c, 14c; Rolf Nussbaumer 11t; Charlie Summers 11bl.
Shutterstock: aarbois front cover cr; Digital Blue 5b; Erin Donalson 12c, 13bl, 15bl, 17bl, 19bl, 21cl; Anton Foltin 6bcl, 7c, 8bcl, 10bcl, 12bcl, 14bcl, 18bc, 20bl, 23t; Martin Froyda 18c; inge hogenbijl 20-21bg; JeniFoto 4; Konstantnin 2, 6t; Maksimilian 22b; NowhereLand Photography 9c; Charles T Peden 10c, 10bcr, 11br, 12bcr, 14bcr, 16br, 18br, 20br; Jay Pierstorff 23br; Tom Roche 1; Stefan Scarf front cover cl; Nattawit Sronrachrudee 6bl, 8bl, 10bl,12bl, 14bl, 16bl, 18bl, 20cl; tntphototravis 5t; Barbara Vallance front cover bc; Milan Zygmunt 22t.

Every attempt has been made to clear copyright. Should there be any inadvertent omission please apply to the publisher for rectification.

Library and Archives Canada Cataloguing in Publication

Title: Who ate the snake? : a desert food chain / Sarah Ridley.
Names: Ridley, Sarah, 1963- author.
Description: Series statement: Follow the food chain | Previously published: London: Wayland, 2019. | Includes index.
Identifiers: Canadiana (print) 20190195002 |
    Canadiana (ebook) 20190195010 |
    ISBN 9780778771432 (hardcover) |
    ISBN 9780778771470 (softcover) |
    ISBN 9781427124548 (HTML)
Subjects: LCSH: Desert ecology—Juvenile literature. |
    LCSH: Food chains (Ecology)—Sonoran Desert—Juvenile literature.
Classification: LCC QH541.5.D4 R53 2020 | DDC j577.54—dc23

Library of Congress Cataloging-in-Publication Data

Names: Ridley, Sarah, 1963- author.
Title: Who ate the snake?: a desert food chain / Sarah Ridley.
Description: New York : Crabtree Publishing Company, 2020. |
    Series: Follow the food chain | Includes index.
Identifiers: LCCN 2019043449 (print) | LCCN 2019043450 (ebook) |
    ISBN 9780778771432 (hardcover) |
    ISBN 9780778771470 (paperback) |
    ISBN 9781427124548 (ebook)
Subjects: LCSH: Food chains (Ecology)--Juvenile literature. |
    Desert ecology--Juvenile literature.
Classification: LCC QH541.15.F66 R538 2020 (print) | LCC QH541.15.
    F66 (ebook) | DDC 577.54--dc23
LC record available at https://lccn.loc.gov/2019043449
LC ebook record available at https://lccn.loc.gov/2019043450

Crabtree Publishing Company

www.crabtreebooks.com   1–800–387–7650
Published by Crabtree Publishing Company in 2020

First published in Great Britain in 2019 by Wayland
Copyright ©Hodder and Stoughton, 2019

All rights reserved. No part of this publication may be reproduced, stored in a retrieval system or be transmitted in any form or by any means, electronic, mechanical, photocopying, recording, or otherwise, without the prior written permission of Crabtree Publishing Company.

Printed in the U.S.A./012020/CG20191115

Published in Canada
Crabtree Publishing
616 Welland Ave.
St. Catharines, Ontario
L2M 5V6

Published in the United States
Crabtree Publishing
PMB 59051
350 Fifth Avenue, 59th Floor
New York, New York 10118

CONTENTS

Food for life

All living things need food to give them **energy** to live. Plants make their own food using water, air, soil, and energy from sunlight.

Cacti and other plants grow in hot, dry **deserts** where there is plenty of sunshine, but not much rain.

Animals cannot make their own food so they have to eat plants, animals, or both.

A gila woodpecker is eating **nectar** from a cactus flower. Can you spot the bee also coming for a drink?

This roadrunner is about to eat a lizard.

Plants and animals are linked together by many different **food chains**. It all depends on what eats what. This book looks at a desert food chain in the United States.

The start of the food chain

Plants are at the start, or bottom, of every desert food chain. This desert food chain starts with a prickly pear cactus. It grows in the Sonoran Desert in Arizona.

← The spiky spines on the cactus pads protect it from animals.

↓ In a food chain, an arrow shows the food energy moving from one living thing to another.

Like all plants, a cactus makes its own food using energy from sunlight, air, water, and the soil. It stores water in its stem and pads. A cactus produces flowers, fruit, and seeds.

? ? ?

Who ate the cactus flower?

A cactus bee ate parts of the cactus flower.

She sucked up the nectar inside the flower and collected its **pollen**. She brought the pollen back to her nest to feed to the young bees.

This cactus bee has dots of yellow pollen stuck to her back legs and body.

?

Some of the pollen brushes off onto the next cactus flower the bee visits. This allows the flower to make fruit and seeds.

Other bees, beetles, bats, and birds, such as this hummingbird, also eat nectar from cactus flowers.

Who ate the cactus fruit?

A cottontail rabbit ate the prickly pear cactus fruit. The rabbit also nibbled the green pads of the cactus to get the water stored inside.

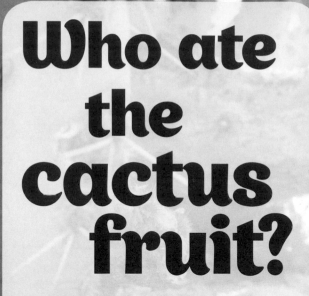

Lots of other animals like to eat prickly pear fruit. They include birds, lizards, rock squirrels, and people.

Golden-fronted woodpecker →

↓ Rock squirrel

↓ Spiny lizard

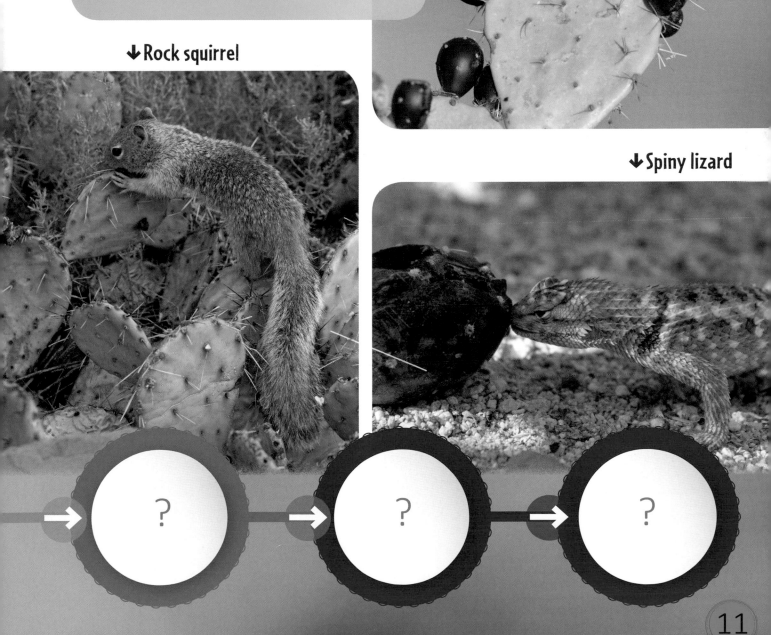

? → ? → ?

Who ate the rabbit?

A rattlesnake ate the rabbit.

The snake waited for the rabbit to get close to it. Then, it darted out and bit the rabbit with its deadly **fangs**.

Like all snakes, a western diamondback rattlesnake can open its jaws very wide to swallow animals. It is a **predator** that hunts other animals for food. The animals it hunts are called **prey**. It also eats mice, rats, and birds.

A western diamondback rattlesnake swallows a wood rat. It will not need to eat again for weeks.

Who ate the rattlesnake?

A roadrunner killed and ate the rattlesnake.

It grabbed the snake, slammed it against the ground, and then ate it.

It is dangerous for a roadrunner to attack a rattlesnake. If the bird can hold the snake's head, the snake cannot use its fangs.

This roadrunner is eating a beetle.

Roadrunners eat both plants and animals. They eat fruit and seeds, as well as insects, lizards, small birds, and mice. They can run very fast on the ground, but will also fly to escape danger.

Who ate the roadrunner?

A coyote ate the roadrunner.

The coyote spotted the roadrunner eating the rattlesnake. The bird ran away, but the coyote ran faster. It caught the roadrunner and ate it.

Coyotes will eat whatever they can find. In the desert, they eat cactus fruit, insects, and small animals, such as rabbits and birds. Coyotes also eat snakes.

This coyote is catching a small animal by pouncing, or jumping, on it.

Who ate the coyote?

A coyote can live for 10 to 14 years in the Sonoran Desert. It is at the top of this desert food chain.

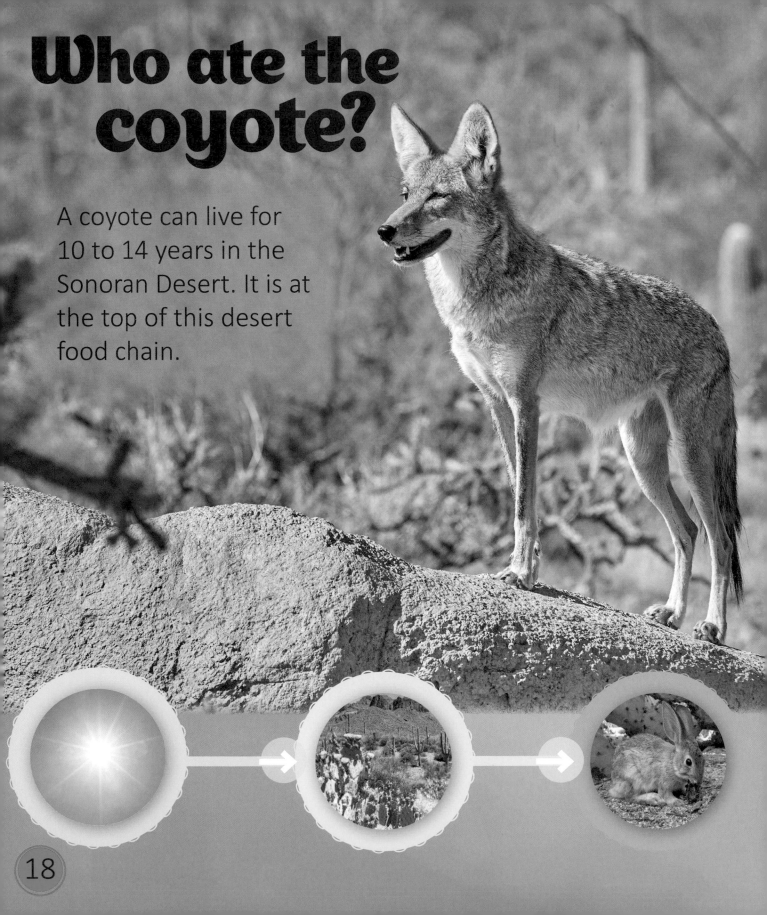

This coyote grew old and died. Others get hit by cars or are shot by hunters. Animals will eat parts of its dead body until all that is left are its bones. Slowly, the bones break down to become part of the soil.

A bald eagle has come to eat this dead coyote.

Follow a desert food chain

There are many different food chains in deserts. They all start with energy from the Sun that is made into food by plants. Animals eat the plants, other animals, or both.

Can you remember the links of the
desert food chain shown in this book?
The answers are at the bottom of
the page.

Desert links

What eats what in a food chain depends on the food chain's location. There are deserts all over the world, including the Arctic and Antarctic. Plants in an Arctic desert food chain include grasses and lichens. Animals include mosquitoes, snowy owls, hares, caribou, and wolves.

Snowy owl

There are many threats to desert food chains. More people living in the Sonoran Desert is one. People build roads and homes. They use groundwater, or water deep underground. This leaves less water for plants such as cacti.

Cactus wren

If there are fewer cacti, there will be less food for animals higher up the food chain.

Useful words

desert A place with very little rain

energy The ability to move and do work. Food energy keeps a living thing alive and allows it to move, breathe, or work in some other way.

fangs Sharp, hollow teeth. Snakes use fangs to inject poison into their prey.

food chain The plants and animals linked together by what eats what

nectar A sweet liquid made inside flowers to attract insects. Nectar is food for bees, insects, and other animals.

pollen A powder made by the male part of a flower

predator An animal that eats other animals

prey Animals that are hunted by predators for food

Index